What others are saying about Ezekial's Vision of the Church Today!

This book sets the tone for recognizing the Laodicean nature that the end time church has taken on. While reading it, you will sense the sound of alarm as the watchman on the wall sounds her trumpet.

Pastor J. Edward Sharp TH. D
River of Life Church

Wow, what a unique and fresh view of an incredible book! In her book Sammie reminded me of the great importance of Ezekiel's words, not only to the people of his day, but to God's people, everyday.

Pastor Rusty Foley
Waters Edge Assembly of God Church

Sammie is a woman after Gods own heart, and this book will help you to discover that same passion for yourself. Read this book, take it to heart, and see what God has in store for you, if you will only follow her advice.

C. E. Sebastian
Retired Junior High Science Teacher

Ezekiel's Vision
of the
Church Today

Ezekiel's Vision *of the* Church Today

Sammie Tubaugh

Tate Publishing
& Enterprises

Tate Publishing is committed to excellence in the publishing industry. Our staff of highly trained professionals, including editors, graphic designers, and marketing personnel, work together to produce the very finest books available. The company reflects the philosophy established by the founders, based on Psalms 68:11,

"The Lord Gave The Word And Great Was The Company Of Those Who Published It."

If you would like further information, please contact us:
1.888.361.9473 | www.tatepublishing.com
Tate Publishing & Enterprises, llc | 127 E. Trade Center Terrace Mustang, Oklahoma 73064 USA

Ezekiel's Vision of the Church Today
Copyright © 2007 by Savilla A. Tubaugh. All rights reserved.

This title is also available as a Tate Out Loud product.
Visit www.tatepublishing.com for more information

No part of this publication may be reproduced, stored in a retrieval system or transmitted in any way by any means, electronic, mechanical, photocopy, recording or otherwise without the prior permission of the author except as provided by USA copyright law.

Scripture quotations marked "KJV" are taken from the *Holy Bible, King James Version,* Cambridge, 1769. Used by permission. All rights reserved.

Book design copyright © 2007 by Tate Publishing, LLC. All rights reserved.
Cover design by Chris Webb
Interior design by Jacob Crissup

Published in the United States of America
ISBN: 978-1-6024711-8-4

07.04.11

TABLE OF CONTENTS

Introduction	11
Chapter 1 *The Defiled Church Today*	15
Chapter 2 *A Praying Church*	29
Chapter 3 *The Real Church*	43
Chapter 4 *Steps and Conditions*	55
Chapter 5 *The Inner Court or Sanctuary*	61
Chapter 6 *The Unfaithful Priests*	69
Chapter 7 *The Zadok Priests*	75
Chapter 8 *Conclusion*	83

"And the Lord said unto me, Son of man, mark well, and behold with thine eyes, and hear with thine ears all that I say unto thee concerning all the ordinances of the house of the Lord, and all the laws thereof: and mark well the entering in of the house, with every going forth of the sanctuary. And thou shall say to the rebellious, even to the house of Israel, Thus saith the Lord God; O ye house of Israel, let it suffice you of all your abominations, in that ye have brought into my sanctuary strangers, uncircumcised in heart, and uncircumcised in flesh, to be in my sanctuary, to pollute it, even my house, when ye offer my bread, the fat and the blood, and they have broken my covenant because of all your abominations. And ye have not kept the charge of mine holy things: but ye have set keepers of my charge in my sanctuary for yourselves."

Ezekiel 44: 5–8

INTRODUCTION

The day I sat down and read Ezekiel 43–47, I didn't realize God was going to speak to me and show me so much and want me to write about it. After I read all this, God began to open his word to me. First he said, "These are my Steps and Conditions to enter into Praise and Worship with me." I am a Holy God and I expect a holy people to worship me but they have gone far from me and they don't even know it.

In Ezekiel 43:10, He said, "Show the house to the house of Israel, that they maybe ashamed of their iniquities: and let them measure the pattern, and if they be ashamed of all that they have done, shew them the form of the house, and the fashion thereof, and the goings out thereof, and the comings in thereof, and all the forms thereof, and all the ordinances thereof, and all the forms thereof, and all the laws thereof: and write it in their sight, that they may keep the whole form thereof, and all the ordinances thereof, and do them." This is the law of the house, because my church or bride, has become so defiled, that people laugh and turn away from her rather than coming to her for help. He said, "I want to teach you these conditions and you will tell my people."

As I began to study these chapters, I was amazed at how far most churches today have gone from God. I was amazed at the requirements God has for us to enter into Praise and Worship.

Before we go any farther, I pray you sit down with the word of God and begin to read chapters 43 through 47 of Ezekiel and let God speak to you, then read this through from the beginning to end and then reread Ezekiel, and let God show you, too. Maybe it will even be more than what is here on paper.

Now as we begin to talk about defilement of the church, we must also look at Revelation chapters 2 and 3 (KJV) where God talks about each of the seven churches. In chapter 1, verse 3, God says, "Blessed is He that readeth, and they which are written therein: for the time is at hand."

Now every church, as He begins to speak, He says, "I know thy works." Now if he said in Ezekiel we were defiled and polluted and we aren't right with him then in Revelation, he talks to His churches about their works. We had better look closely at this and see what he is saying to

Ezekiel's Vision of the Church Today

us. "He that hath an ear, let him hear what the Spirit saith unto the churches."

Each church he speaks to, except Sardis and Laodicea, he tells, first, what he sees good about them, then what he has against them, and then if they listen and overcome the bad parts what they shall inherit in the Kingdom.

Now in Sardis, he tells them they use to be alive and active, on fire for him.

Now they are dead and they don't even know it sounds a little bit like Ezekiel. In Sardis, God says he hasn't found any of their works to be perfect before God. He asks them to repent, then he says if they will overcome they shall even enter the Kingdom of Heaven.

Now the church of Laodicea thinks she is OK. Rich increased with goods, having need of nothing, God says, "She is poor, naked, blind totally miserable and don't even know it, she needs eye salve to see." This is the defiled church of today that Ezekiel had the vision of. Let us now look at the church today.

CHAPTER 1
The Defiled Church Today

The church today is becoming so much like the world it is hard sometimes to tell them apart. God wants separated people, a peculiar people. The church is not to be of the world, it is only in the world. It is to be without spot or wrinkle, and no blemishes. In Ezekiel 8, God took the prophet to the church and showed him in the spirit what the pastors or elders were doing and imagining in their thoughts. Their minds were so dirty and vile they thought God wouldn't see it. Today is no different. Those same thoughts and acts are being done in our churches today and this is a great abomination to God. How can they call themselves men of God and do the corrupt things that is going on now in our churches. Do they think God can't see what is going on inside them and inside the churches?

The churches today have so much sin and disease it is

hard to tell them from the world. The world looks at us and wants to know where are the miracles they heard about? The parting of the Red sea, David, when he slew Goliath. The world is like Goliath, the uncircumcised Philistine, defying the armies of God.

We are like King Saul, so weak, no strength, no faith, that we let them taunt us and make us look like God is the weakling and the devil is the strong one. The Word says, "Greater is He that is in me than He that is in the world." Where are our David's today?

Most of us don't know the word well enough to slay the enemy with it or have the faith that we need in God to make it through the day some days, let alone know it and use it to trample the enemy underfoot for a lifetime. God says all we need is faith the size of a grain of mustard seed to move mountains, but in order to apply it you must know it. It's like when you buy something that needs assembled, first you read the directions, then assemble it step by step. Not us, we run out with one scripture and hope to defeat the devil. Why not read the directions, apply them all, and then maybe we can become the overcomer rather than be overcome.

We are a lot like the seven sons of Sceva, in Acts 19: 13–16. When they tried to cast out the evil spirit, and the spirit said, "Jesus I know and Paul I know but who are you?" Does Satan's world know you? We are such a pitiful Bride.

I really feel God is angry with us and He says, "How long do I put up with you, you perverse and wicked generation?" Yet God said, "Peter on this rock {of Revelation} I will build my church and the gates of hell shall not prevail against it." Satan and the hordes of hell are beating on every church door and every believer's heart today trying to prevail and doing a pretty good job of it. I ask again does Satan's world know you? Does he live at your house? Does he come often to visit because you are turning his world up side down with your prayers?

Where is the church that God was talking about to Peter? Have you seen it somewhere and if you have, why are you not in it, defeating Satan? Satan is already defeated because God said he was. It is nothing we do, but what knowing, speaking, and living the word will do. Christ's shed blood at Calvary gives us the right, and we can follow Christ's example by defeating him with the spoken word. Satan cannot cross the blood line of Christ. Draw the line with him and don't allow him any room to maneuver in. Remember we are in a warfare but Christ said, "The battle is not ours it is the Lords."

Twice now I have had a dream of Satan coming to me. Each time he knows who I am and asks me if I know him and who I am coming against with my prayers? I say "yes" and the battle is on, but he can't cross the blood line of Jesus Christ. He is a defeated foe. Each time he speaks I give him back the word, and he backs up. He knows he is no match for the word but yet he knows the word far better than we do and most of the time he will defeat us with the word rather than us defeating him with it. God didn't go to the cross and suffer death and the sins of this earth for that uncircumcised Philistine to win over us. We are more than Conquerors through Jesus Christ, our Lord.

God said, "His house is a house of prayer." How many churches do you know that advocate prayer? Most bless the service, the offering, and the end of the service, that's it. When was the last time you went to a prayer meeting? A prayer meeting where you pray. Most Christians today don't even know how to pray. Pastors need to teach you how to do spiritual warfare in the heavenlies through prayer. Did you know that most Christians today won't even bless their food in public for fear of ridicule from people. We need to know how to bind the enemy hand and foot, so we are not caught in his snares and traps. The Lord said, "What you bind on earth he will bind in heaven." We are in a war here, folks, just like our military is in Iraq. There are both Physical and Spiritual wars and how we pray about each one will determine the outcome of both.

The church today can't stand up straight anymore. She has bowed to so many man made rules and government rules that she is staying in a bent over position, just in case some other wind of doctrine comes along; she is already bowed down. We need to be like Shadrach, Meshach, and Abednego. We will not bow nor even bend to you, O King Nebuchadnezzar, even if the furnace of affliction is really hot, but no, we sometimes bow so fast we fall on our face. We should be on our face all right, but in a prone position before God crying out for him to save his people, pastors, and the church. We need a great revival today.

When Jesus ministered on this earth, he never went anywhere or did anything before praying first. He spent long periods of time in prayer. He said, "He did the will of the Father." He did what he saw his Father do. I was thanking God the other day for the earthly father he gave me. He taught me how to trust my heavenly Father. When my father was alive and I was a little girl, I wanted to go everywhere with him and do everything with him. The same is true today; I don't want to go anywhere or do anything without my heavenly Father. When things go wrong, who else is there that cares. God said, "Cast your cares on me for I careth for you." We as a church and the Bride of Christ need to spend so much time with him that we know him very intimately. How can we help save this earth from hell if we don't know the one who conquered hell? The only way to know someone is to spend time with them.

The church isn't spending the time with the Father like it should be. When Christ was here he spent a lot of time with the Father and then the disciples, teaching them. One thing he taught them was how to pray. If the church doesn't teach you, get in the word and ask God to show you how. The Lord's Prayer is the perfect prayer to pray.

First. You begin with Praise, "Our Father who art in heaven Hallowed be thy name."

Spend some time giving Him praise for who he is, Holy, Holy, Holy is He.

Second. "Thy Kingdom come thy will be done." Pray it first for you, so you are in right relationship with him. 2. Pray it second for your loved ones, so they can be saved and ready to go to heaven. 3. Pray it for your church, so she will be where she is to be with God. 4. Pray it for your nation, so she will make the right decisions for us as a people.

Third. "Give us this day our daily bread." After you have given over to God's will all these things and made His Kingdom your priority, then you ask for your needs to be met for everyday.

Fourth. "Forgive us our debts as we forgive our debtors." This means we must forgive in love everything that someone does to us. If we can't do this, God, the Father, can't forgive us of the things we have done against him. This is not easy but as you follow this and pray it always, it will begin to come easier for you.

Fifth. "And lead us not into temptation, but deliver us from evil." Pray a hedge of protection around you first, then your family, home, job, and possessions. Put on the armor

Ezekiel's Vision of the Church Today

of God along with the hedge of protection and Satan will have a tough time touching you. This is power in prayer.

Sixth. "For thine is the Kingdom and Power and Glory forever." Amen. This is Praise again. We always begin and end with Praise to our Heavenly Father.

Ask God how to defeat Satan. He will teach you. God said in Luke 10: 18–19, "I beheld Satan as lightning fall from heaven, Behold I give you power to tread on serpents and scorpions and over all power of the enemy and nothing shall by no means hurt you." The church today is taking the sting of the fiery darts of Satan and allowing them to destroy her. Some of the people we call Christians today doesn't want to hear about a Satan or hell, only the good things of God.

People, Satan and his world is real and a lot of people are going to go to hell if we don't do something about it. We are in a war with the hordes of hell. It is a spiritual war not a physical war like we are in now with Iraq. Our war is not carnal but mighty through God to the pulling down of strong holds. {Strong hold means Fortified Places.}

Satan has built a fort around these places in our lives. We must pull them down through spiritual warfare prayer. Satan has them hidden behind things like imagination. The things we can dwell on in our minds and heart, like anger, witchcraft, same as rebellion, our tongue, in the things we speak. We must fight with God's weapons, not ours. God help us not to neglect so great a salvation.

What are God's people and the churches doing about the cries of so many innocent babies being aborted today? Not much, will we stand blameless before God for this? I say, NO! NO! and NO! We the church should be seeing these signs and know Jesus is coming soon. We should be on our knees crying out daily for this world that allows such things to go on. Even if the courts of Justice advocate this, we need to pray for them. How neglectful are we. When we stand before God what will our answer be? Well, the courts of our government said, "It was ok, God, I am only one person." What a cop-out. We will be held accountable. When God's word say's it is wrong, then it is wrong, end of story. When people say it isn't a real person, yet God says, "I knew you before you were even conceived in your mother's womb." Jeremiah 1:5

We the church should have compassion for these people. We should tell them the truth, preach it from the pulpits. Instead we have companionship with the world. "A companion is someone you walk along side and hold hands with, have the same interests and desires, want to see the same out come of things." God said, "You are in the world, not part of it, be ye a separated people." Romans 8 says, "Walk after the Spirit not the flesh for to be carnally minded is death, but to be spiritually minded is life and peace."

Let's talk about the defilement of the church where homosexuality is concerned. The churches that are ordaining them, how will you answer God? It goes against God's word. In Colossians 3:5 it says, "Mortify therefore your members," which means put to death inordinate affection. I Corinthians 6:9 says, "Know ye not that the unrighteous shall not inherit the kingdom of God." "Be not deceived: neither fornicators, nor idolaters, nor adulterers, nor effeminate {homosexuals}, nor abusers of themselves with mankind."

God said, "Be not deceived." The sad part is some are very deceived. How are you only believing and preaching some of the word? God said, "Don't add to the word or take away from the word or you would be judged accordingly." Why do you think Sodom and Gomorrah were destroyed? Wake up church. You're believing a lie from the father of lies, Satan and his unholy kingdom. God will call you workers of iniquity and say, "Depart from me I never knew you."

What about fasting, are we in defilement there also? God's word says, "These things come about by much fasting and prayer." God wants a people that will fall on their face with sincere hearts and begin to fast, the fasts of the old days. In Zechariah 7:5 God asks, "Have you fasted to me or for yourselves, to help bring my will about or only to prosper you and look good before men." Those fasts mean nothing to God.

In Zechariah 7: 9–12, God tells the people why to fast.

Verse 9: "To execute true judgment, and shew mercy and compassions every man to his brother:"

Verse 10: "And oppress not the widow, not the fatherless, the stranger, not the poor; and don't anyone imagine evil against his brother in your heart."

Verse11: "But they refused to hear, they jerked the hand of God from their shoulders, stopped their ears so as not to hear and made their hearts hard lest they hear the law of God."

Verse12: "They made their hearts as adamant stone."

That is pretty hard. Because of this the Lord sent a great wrath. Are we guilty of this ourselves? Stubborn, hard hearted, not wanting to hear the words of God. We had better be very careful what we are doing, people, God is still sovereign.

The shepherds need to begin to show by example what praying and fasting will do, if done for the right reasons. If it be of God, you can fast as long as he says to. In Daniel 10:3, Daniel says he fasted for three weeks before his answer came. Do we pray and ask God to call us weeping and fasting for his people and church? Probably not. Oh, to be called of God to pray and fast for his church. It is such an honor, or should be. The church or people, today, fast maybe a meal at a time, pray about five minutes and then wonder why they have no answers. The pastors' are as guilty as the people in this area. In some big churches today, the people never get to see nor talk to the pastor; it is the hireling under him. The only time you see the pastor is on the platform when it is time to preach, then he leaves. The hireling takes over again, so in some instances the underling begins to think he is the pastor but look out, he could be the wolf in shepherds clothing. The devil is clever in using people for his own devices and scatters the sheep in the process. If the sheep is a new convert, they are left vulnerable to the wolf. John 10:10 says, "The thief cometh not but to steal, kill and destroy."

We should be on our face daily lifting up our pastors, fasting for their lives and ministries, remembering the fire the pastors walk through, the people usually follow right behind. The church is the bride of Christ, what better place for Satan to hit hard. If he can destroy the church, and we are the church, he has stopped the hand of God. When the people become hard hearted, God has to wait for us to come to our senses and cry out to him. We are the ones that stop everything from happening. When God begins to give out heeds and warnings and the people, His church does not listen but stop up their ears, then God usually will lift His hand against that church.

It is no wonder the word says, {Mark 13:20–22} "If God didn't shorten the days at the end, even the very elect would be fooled into accepting the Antichrist and the mark of the beast, believing the lies of Satan." {Luke 21:31} God said "When we see these things beginning to take place look up for our redemption is nigh."

Now Passed in Congress, a Bill {S.578}, Report No. {103–111}, "To protect the Free exercise of religion," on the surface it is a good bill and does not discriminate against anyone, which is the way it is suppose to be. We need to pay attention how our government writes these things up. It gives Satan worshipers the right to be recognized as a church, with the right to sacrifice animals for religious ceremonies, using their shed blood. Remember Satan always has an imitation for anything that God has. Jesus shed his life's blood for our sins. The devil cannot use this precious blood; he has to use animals for he has no chance for repentance or forgiveness.

If the church takes her rightful place, once again, and stands up against sin in all places and begins to preach against it rather than condoning it, we will see changes made. Don't forget our church maybe defiled right now, but if we pray, fast, and seek God for her and our country, I know He will listen. Did He not set atop the hill of Jerusalem and say of her, "O Jerusalem, Jerusalem thou that killest the prophets and stonest them which are sent unto you, how often would I have gathered thy children together, even as a hen doth her chickens under her wings, and ye would not," Matthew 23:37. Did he not create us with his own hands? Does he not love us still? Would he not gather us also as he would of Jerusalem? He cares so much for us let us not kill our prophets or stone who God sends to us to give us warnings.

God says in Ezekiel 43, He would not put up with the defilement of His church any more. We have polluted it long enough. God is trying to show us here, in these chapters, how to go from the defiled and polluted to the entering in of His Presence in His church with Praise and Worship. Let us listen to what he is saying and follow the conditions laid out in the word so the Shechinah Glory of God will fall on our services and we will enter into his glorious presence. That we will be the righteous and holy bride he is coming for. He said in Revelation 3:20, "Behold I stand at the door and knock, if any man hear my voice and open the door, I will come in and sup with him and he with me."

This defiled church of today can be likened to the church of Laodicea. "Repent fully," He said. Get on fire and be the overcomer, then we can sit with Him around his throne and join into the marriage supper of the Lamb. Let us hear what the spirit is saying in Ezekiel and in Revelation. Wake up, not slumber ourselves into hell; but repent, for the kingdom of heaven is at hand. God will only give us so many chances before He shuts the door of the Ark of Safety. He is giving us that chance now.

CHAPTER 2
A Praying Church

Since we have talked about prayer and the church not praying like it should and the Lord's Prayer being the perfect prayer to pray, I am going to talk about this and show you how to pray this prayer.

Prayer is what gets God's attention. You, the people, are what he uses to accomplish his purpose on earth. Nothing is done without it. It is like a thunder bolt when you begin to come against hell and the enemies of the cross. All through the Word it talks about prayer. You will be surprised when you begin to pray this way. Mountains begin to move and you see unmovable problems begin to dissolve right before your eyes, but remember you will also get the attention of hell. Jesus said, "The gates of hell would not prevail against the church." If you have a praying church then you will see great things happen.

In the Greek, the word prayer is translated to mean Worship. You begin to worship God in your praying. This means there is not much God would not do for you, as a Church or a person. So let's begin and I will try to show you by my example how to pray. Now this is not a set prayer, it is showing you how you can pray or begin to learn how to pray. In the garden when the Lord took the disciples with him so he could pray about going to the cross, He bled great drops of blood in doing this. He asked the disciples, "Could you not pray with me for one hour?" Now this is hard to do but if you start slowly and add more time each day to you prayers, you will be surprised how easy it can become. The more time you spend with the Lord, the closer your walk with him becomes. Let's learn how to pray the Lord's Prayer now.

First: You begin with Praise: "Our Father who art in heaven Hallowed be thy name."

Father, I praise you for your holiness. I praise you for who you are. You are an awesome God, worthy of all our praise. Holy, Holy, Holy are you. The slain Lamb of God, you took my condemnation to the cross for me. You wore my pain and suffering so I wouldn't have to. I glory in you, Lord. Only you are worthy to be called my Lord and my God. There is no other God above you. I worship you, Lion of Judah. The one who closed the lion's mouth, in the den with Daniel. Would you do no less for me? You are a great and mighty God. Worthy is the Lamb.

Second: "Thy kingdom come thy will be done on earth as it is in heaven."

1. Pray for yourself first:

Lord, I want your perfect will in my life. I want to do on earth what you have called me to do. I want to go where no man has ever gone with you before. I don't want to walk someone else's walk. Take me to a higher place in you, a deeper place with you, a place of cleansing and purification. Take me into that special, special place where I can hear your voice and get direction. I want to be consumed in the fire of the Holy Ghost. Show me your glory, Lord, let nothing be left of me but the image of you. Help me to show compassion that I might receive the same. Transform me and renew me in the spirit. Show me your ways. This is my hearts cry, to love you more. Help me to be strong each day. Help me to pray for mine enemies to love even the unlovable.

Help me to pray and touch lives, change me Lord, if no one else needs to be changed, I do. I want to be the image of you. Teach me how to wait on you that I will learn patience. Wake me up in the night to pray, if necessary.

Let me be a vessel of use that I can rattle the gates of hell. Put a hedge of thorns and briers around me that no fiery darts of the enemy can penetrate so I will be protected to do your bidding. Help me to stand in the gap when there is no other to do it. I want a heart after you to care about the things you care about not my own selfish ways. Tear down any and all fortified places strongholds of my heart so the enemy won't have a hold of me in any way, so I may pray for your purpose and reason. Take me to a depth I have never known before, to walk where I have never walked before. Help me to defeat the enemy for my family and church's sake. Take my life completely for you. Amen.

2. Now for my spouse:

For my husband, because he is one with me, cover him to keep him in all your ways. Help him to be a strong tower in my life. One that I can always depend on, knowing he is who you have chosen for my partner, to love and cherish, to lift up and to encourage. Help me to always know your love for him; it is so much more than mine. Your plan for his life will include me in every thing, so guard us and protect us. Help him to keep your holy word and apply the directions for success in our home and life. Help him to be prosperous in every thing he puts his hand to, so we are a blessing in the lives of other people. Guard his thoughts and the intent of his heart to keep the lusts of the flesh out.

Ezekiel's Vision of the Church Today

Let him become the man you know he can be both physical and spiritual. Bless his coming in and his going out and make him the head and not the tail. Show him how to run his business the way you know it should be run. Guard him against destruction that the enemy could use for his gain and our loss. Give him a heart after you and let him begin to look at things the way you do. Help us to have a long and glorious life together and with you. Protect his life always and let him to be an example that other people want to copy after, because he follows after you and is becoming the exact image of you. Let him love you and then me above all others, and keep our marriage on your solid rock of security that we will be unmovable. I will praise you for it this day. Amen

3. Now for your loved ones:

Father, I pray for my family and your will be done in their lives for they are lost and on their way to a devil's hell. Save them, please, and open their eyes, that they may see; cause their hard hearts to soften toward you and show them their need for salvation. I bind the enemy that the strong places in their lives will be torn down. Unstop their ears to hear what the spirit is calling unto them. Send some one into their lives that they will listen, too.

Now speak to the devil out loud. Satan, I bind you and your demons that have my family in your clutches, the blood line of Jesus has been drawn and you can't cross it. Back up and take your hands off my family. I command every assignment and contract against my family to be broken off them, and every demon touching them cast back to the pits of hell where they came from never to touch them again. When you come against what is mine, devil, you are coming against Jesus Christ himself, for I am a child of the most high God, so take your filthy hands off them. The word says, "What I bind on earth shall be bound in heaven and what I loose on earth shall be loosed in heaven." Devil, you are bound. I loose the Holy Ghost of God and I dispatch angels from heaven to go to my family and draw them then to God. They will be saved, they will denounce you and your unholy demons, for I proclaim it now in the heavenlies, take your hands off and leave. Father God, I pray you surround my family with so much protection from the enemy that they will be able to hear and see clearly what the enemy has done to them this whole time, and be able to repent of their sins and receive salvation for their souls this day. Amen

4. Now for your pastor:

Father, I pray now for my pastor. Keep your hand upon him Lord don't allow the enemy to distract him from your will. Put protection all around him to keep his mind pure, for he is only human. Keep him safe from the darts of the

Ezekiel's Vision of the Church Today

enemy and give him a clean heart and a right spirit. Protect him from the lusts of the flesh in this world and keep him pure and holy before you.

Father, the load he carries for his church is awesome and every soul rests on his shoulders. The weight can be so heavy at times, please lighten the load. Keep his mind on you to hear your still small voice when you speak. Don't let him listen to every voice speaking but only to yours and the ones you want him to hear.

Don't allow him on any road that leads to destruction. Let his heart be after you and the things you have called him to do. Let him want his church to see the glory of God fall, and let his desire be to cry after you. Put an unstoppable flow of the Holy Spirit in him to carry over to the congregation. Let him preach the pure word of God. Let him cry out daily for the holiness of God in his life and for the congregation. Teach him how to use the weapons of God for his church. His responsibility as the man of God for this hour is unbelievable so show him your ways and your concepts, line on line and precept on precept. Don't let him vary to left or right but keep him focused on you and what you need him to accomplish to bring about your will for your church.

Lord, you open what no man can shut and you shut what no man can open. Shut up the world around him so he will see in the spirit as you see. Open up to him the deep and awesome things of you so he can feed the sheep the word for this hour. Don't allow any power to take over his life except the power of the Holy Ghost and make him a Zadok Priest, holy and acceptable unto you, worthy to take his congregation into the Holy of Holies. Take care of this man you have placed as shepherd and guide in my life to bring about my change to go from glory to glory and enter into your presence that we may reside with you there. Amen

5. For your church

Father, help me to pray for your church and let me see her the way you do that I may pray your perfect will. Let our church be a soul saving station for the lost, the lonely, the hurting, and the dying. Help us to see beyond our needs to the needs of others so when they come in off the streets we can minister to them the way you would. Let us not be judgmental for that is your place, not ours. Let us show love beyond degree so when they come they have no reason to leave. We want them to see the love of Jesus for them not condemnation for what they are coming out of. Help us to teach them how to live by the word of God and to remember they are babes in Christ, stumbling and learning, not prefect, as we sometimes think we are. Give us wisdom, Father, in the ministering that will need to be done. Let us be ready to handle every situation with Godly wisdom and prayer. This is your bride and we must prepare now for who you choose to come in not who we choose. Father, help me to see their hearts as you do, not their flesh. At one time I was hard hearted and unlovely, too.

Prepare us to help gather this end time harvest you are getting ready to bring in for she must be pure and holy, cleansed, and sanctified, ready for the marriage supper with you. Let our church be a part of this end time move of God, to see the holiness of God in this latter rain time. Consume us, your church, with the fire of the Holy Ghost that nothing will shake us or move us only the Spirit of the living God. Let our church be known as a house of prayer. Where prayer is taught and lived. Where we, as soldiers in God's army, fight the war in the spirit and in the heavenlies to see the battle's won, even though we might lose some. Teach us to be intercessors for your will to be carried out. Bring us into the unified body of Christ that we are to be in one mind and one accord when we pray. Show us your glory, as your glory falls and consumes us. Set us on fire with an unquenchable thirst for you that we will be holy and acceptable unto you. Thank you for allowing me to be a part of this great move that is coming. I give you praise and glory forever. Amen.

6. Now for your nation.

Father, I pray for our leaders to be lead by your spirit

in every decision they make for this great nation. Give us leaders that follow after you and the concepts of your word. Don't allow world powers to determine the outcome here. You have placed your hand on us to lead the world in peace and freedom. Now give us the leaders to bring about your will. Keep her shores safe and secure that we will always produce freedoms for everyone. Help them to put laws into effect that will be necessary to keep her, the America that you created with the brave and valiant men that first came here to worship, a free country. Help our people to want to be a nation under God once again. Take out the unholy rulers and put in the men who will follow after the things of you and create laws that shadow those belief's for she is the greatest nation on earth and help her leaders to keep her that way.

I pray for the men and women who are there to defend her. Make them strong and diligent in their work and keep them safe at all costs for they are the protectors of our rights and freedoms you put in place. Put men of strong godly characters as leaders in our defense. Let the things of God ring true once again from our halls of Justice. Put your godly principles back in there once again with strong men and women that can carry us through. I thank you, Lord, for this great and wonderful nation we call America. May she always be one nation under God indivisible, with Liberty and Justice for all. Amen

Third: Give us this day our daily bread.

Father, you know each day what I need to see me through but your word says to pray for it so I might learn to stand on the word. I thank you for my job for without it I would have nothing. Thirty-three years ago I needed a job and I asked for one that would last me till I didn't need it anymore. You answered me. I thank you for the food you put on my table every day and the clothes I wear, the home you have provided for me to live in. You have thought of everything.

I pray you pay every bill due in our home with enough left over for other things. I bind the enemy that comes against us to stop the blessing of God. Your word says, "My God shall supply all my needs according to His riches in glory," not might supply, shall supply. I pray for the decisions that have to be made today and that I will make the right ones, and the protection you will give us this day that the enemy can't hurt us. Give me enough to also bless others. Your word proclaims that we can have abundantly above all that we could ask or think.

If someone needs an encouraging word today, allow me to be the vessel used to supply that need for them. Everyone can use a kind word or a smile now and then. Your word says you are the one who gives us power to get wealth. I pray for that power in my husband to sell homes to people that it will supply income every month for us, give him ideas that he may have success today in his business. Provide for our family, Lord, that they may have enough also. Protect our children and grandchildren today and pay their bills. Put food on their table that they be not in need. Your word tells me you will restore what the cankerworm has stolen from us that we may bring our tithes to your house to see the needs meet there, so your blessing will fall on us in this area also. Father, the enemy has robbed us long enough. The word tells me, "To ask and it shall be given, to knock, and the door will be opened to us, seek and we shall find," so from this day forward help me to stand on your word for my needs every day. Amen

Fourth. Forgive us our debts as we forgive our debtors

Father, I owe you so much, more than I could ever pay yet I ask you to forgive me daily for things I do, but for some reason I sometimes have a hard time forgiving other people. Change my heart that I may forgive as you do and I don't see the faults of others when I look at them but only see the good just as you do when you look at us. I am such a brat at times, I need corrected but you do it with mercy and grace not with I told you so's. Help me to see the pain of others as I myself hurt that I will have compassion for them rather then condemnation. You went to Calvary for their souls as much as you did for mine.

Ezekiel's Vision of the Church Today

Who am I to think I am judge yet I do it freely? God forgive me and teach me in your ways. If anyone owes me anything and can't pay, help me to remember there are times I owe and can't pay either. Teach me mercy for I need it desperately. Give me a loving and forgiving heart to show that mercy to others, to love the unlovable for I was once there myself. Create in me a clean heart and a right spirit that others see you in me. Amen.

Fifth: Lead us not into temptation but deliver us from evil.

Father, help me every day to put on the armor of God to protect me from the evil that surrounds me. Don't let me walk down the road of despair and destruction that awaits me. The snares and traps set for me by the devil is real for I know his job is to rob me, kill me, if possible, and totally destroy me.

When temptations come my way, Lord, help me to see it for what it is and to stop it before I get caught up in it. Let me say kind words and to see the good in things to give smiles for frowns and hugs for sadness. I pray that you will show me the hurts of people so I may be an example of you to them.

Father, I know there is more evil in this world than good most times, but help me to shun it and only see the good and lovely, for your word says to think on these things. The evil and temptations of this world are around me every day. I am the one who must choose which path I take and who I will be lead by. Oh Lord, show me always what to do. Don't let me turn left or right but to keep on the straight and narrow road that leads to you and deliver me from evil. Amen.

Sixth: For thine is the kingdom and the power and the glory forever.

Now we end with praise.

For this kingdom, Father, is yours and ours to come with all power and glory, I thank you for it and praise you, Lord, for the rights and privileges you give me to pray this prayer. I give you all glory for you are worthy to receive our praise and worship. Amen.

You can become a prayer warrior for God if you follow this prayer. He taught his disciples how to pray by using it so it must be very effective. These are only sample prayers; you put your own words in for each step and use it every day. The word says in James 5:16, "The effectual fervent prayer of a righteous man availeth much."

I pray this will help you to see what we need to be doing in our prayer life to bring the church and us back to our first love so our defilement is gone and he will say to us, "Well done thy good and faithful servant."

CHAPTER 3
The Real Church

Now, in the first chapter we talked about the defiled or polluted church. This is the vision that God gave Ezekiel of his church and it is still relevant today.

Now, the church is supposed to be a refuge, a place of safety, a place where peace, joy, love, and happiness abounds. The church is to go into all the world and preach the gospel, cast out devils, heal the sick, set the captives free, open prison doors of depression, and oppression, open blind eyes, unstop deaf ears and teach the holiness of God.

The church is to teach the complete Bible, not bits and pieces. If the word says, "I am the same yesterday, today and forever," how can you then teach certain things are not functioning today?

Some teach, once saved always saved. In Ezekiel 18:24 it says, "But when the righteous turneth away from his righteousness, and commiteth iniquity, and doeth according to all the abominations that the wicked man doeth, shall he live?" All his righteousness that he hath done shall not be mentioned: in his sin that he hath sinned, in them shall he die. This tells me if a person willfully turns their back on God and gives themselves over to Satan, and denies God to do the worldly things he will die in his sin and no one can change it. All my right living for God before that day or hour will not be counted for me as righteousness. I am not once saved always saved. For without true repentance I can give up my salvation. Read Hebrew's 6: 4–8. Now this is in the New Testament under grace not under the law in the Old Testament.

Hebrew 6: 4: "For it is impossible for those who were once enlightened, and have tasted of the heavenly gift, and were made partakers of the Holy Ghost,"

Verse 5: "And have tasted the good word of God, and the powers of the world to come,"

Verse 6: "If they shall fall away, to renew them again unto repentance: seeing they crucify to themselves the Son of God afresh, and put him to an open shame."

Verse 7: "For the earth which drinketh in the rain that cometh oft upon it, and bringeth forth herbs meet for them by whom it is dressed, receiveth blessing from God."

Verse 8: But that which beareth thorns and briers is rejected, and is nigh unto cursing; whose end is to be burned."

Ezekiel's Vision of the Church Today

If I turn away, and forsake God and my decision of repentance to follow him and go back to the world, I could forever be lost. Philippians 2:12 says, "To work out your own salvation with fear and trembling." Guard your salvation. Don't let others talk you into doing things that will cause you to fall away or cast aside your salvation. Guard it with fear of losing it and it will help keep evil at bay. This will keep your soul from being lost and going to a devil's hell. I know that sometimes serving God is not as easy as some might lead you to believe. It is a glorious walk. It is an exciting walk. Everyday life is not easy and things happen to us and sometimes we bring things on us ourselves, which makes life unpleasant. When we do, we, at times, don't think we can handle the situation so we give up on God and serving him when he is the only one that can bring us through the problem. We should run to him with it instead of away from him. Don't let Satan have free rein with our lives causing us to run to him rather than our Father.

Some churches believe if you sin you can go to a priest or pastor and do penance and be in right standing with God asking for forgiveness through some one other than going to the Father himself. You must ask forgiveness for yourself through Jesus Christ. Jesus Christ is our mediator between you and God our Father. I am not saying a priest or pastor cannot pray for you and ask God to help you get back in right standing with God, but the only forgiveness this man can give is if you have sinned against him. Jesus died on the cross so we could boldly enter into the throne room of God ourselves without the need for another to plead our cause. He is accessible to everyone who calls on his name and repents of their sins. They only need to cry out to him not to another man.

Some churches teach, today, that healing is not for now. It was only when Jesus walked on this earth. Well, if God never changes, then how can you teach that he changed and won't heal today? Nowhere do I read that Jesus quit doing the work of the Father in certain areas because it was for the Old Testament and not for the new? God says, "I change not." Our churches need to teach the whole word of God and not just what they want to. In Revelation 22: 18–19, the word says, "For I testify unto every man that heareth the words of the prophecy of this book, If any man shall add unto these things, God shall add unto him the plagues that are written in this book: and if any man shall take away from the words of the book of this prophecy {or message}, God shall take away his part out of the book of life and out of the holy city, and from the things which are written in this book." Now these are pretty strong words, I don't know if the churches are reading them or not but they had better take close measure of what they are saying and teaching people.

The real church was preaching and teaching daily. I know

that we can't be in church every day, that is impossible for most people but the church is supposed to be working daily to see souls saved. How many of you know people who aren't ready to meet God? Everywhere we go we should ask God to open doors, to give the gospel to someone. Everyone deserves the chance to meet God and live for him. Most of us are very content to do our daily things and never one time tells anyone about God. I am as guilty as anyone. I pray God changes me to be more like him so I won't take anyone's salvation for granted. We are missing the point, folks. The real church wanted everyone to know about what God could do.

God is still in the same business now as he was back then. How many of you believe we must be born again to enter the kingdom of heaven? The Bible says this is what it takes. Most of us can't explain to people how to be saved. It is so simple but most people make it hard. We need to tell people that just going to church is not being saved. Living for God is much more than church. It is a way of life. You meet people who say, "I tried going to church but it was so hard to live that way. I quit." Living for God daily is one of the hardest walks they will ever walk. It should be one of the most glorious and fulfilling walks they will ever go on and we need to tell them that when they become born again. God never said it would be a picnic. He said, "If they persecute me, how much more will they hate and persecute you."

When you get saved or born again you are no longer living for self. Now you have someone to live for. He said, "He would take care of you." I think a lot of our problems with serving God are we only want to read and live the easy parts where he promises to have all these things for us. We don't want to read the parts that make a condition of the promise. There is always a condition before getting to the promise.

Now if the church {you} is doing exactly what is required in the word then God's promises can be stood on with great faith, because God is not a liar. If he wrote it, now he must fulfill His word. Now you can stand on the word till the promise comes, but it may take awhile. We must leave the timing up to God. Here is when faith comes in to play, in Hebrews 11:1, the word says, "Now faith is the substance of things hoped for, the evidence of things not seen." If you could see the answer you wouldn't need faith to see it through. There will always be trials to go through but now we don't have to go alone, God will go and prepare the way for us.

In August of the year 2000, God gave me a poem and I wrote it down and dated it for I knew my Father didn't give me something without reason, here it is.

Life

When I go into the valley of sorrow and despair,
Send as my companions Lord peace and comfort there

Give me peace to walk with me in this valley low,
And when despair raises up, to comfort I will go.

Then on to faith and trust, to lead me out of there,
On the path that you have chosen, without sorrow and despair.

Onward to the mountain top with faith and trust I go,
Climbing ever higher with uncertainty in tow.

As I climb up to the summit, on the mountain top so high,
Faith and trust accompany me, uncertainty is lost.

I look back at the valley I left so long ago,
Knowing without Faith and trust back there I would go.

If some day I do descend back to the valley floor,
I know that peace and comfort will meet me at the door.

Thank you Lord for my companions you send to lead the way,
On this path of life I travel day by day by day.

Sammie Tubaugh

Not long after that I went through a very bad trial. God gave me the peace and comfort to see me through. I am stronger today because of the trials that he allows my walk in life to take and you will be, too, not as you walk there but when it is over you can look back and see where he lead you with his hand to guide you safely to the victory. Remember he is our shepherd. A shepherd always guides the sheep to safe pasture. We must remember his walk was hazardous at times and so will ours be, but we the church need to get in right standing with God.

We need to preach and teach the whole word of God, and begin to pray and fast like never before, then we would see a revival like never before. The church is failing in what she is supposed to be doing. The miracles that you read about in the Bible can be ours again. They are for the Christian not Satan and his hordes of demons, but we are not meeting the conditions.

God says he is coming for a glorious church one who is working when he comes, but most of us as the church don't want to give up anything to do as he wants. The word says in Matthew 22:14, "Many are called but few are chosen." He chooses few because very few say, "God, I love you so much, I'll do anything for you, and if no one else will go or do for you, here am I, send me." He doesn't always have a lot to choose from. When I pray I tell him I am so untrained but I want to serve him any way I can and I don't know what I can do but here am I use me to the best of your ability because I don't have much ability of my own. This is what God is looking for in his church, to be willing and love the ones he sends in. This can start the greatest revival. We must teach love for this was one of the greatest commandments for us to follow. When someone comes in off the street, they are searching for someone to care, for on the streets it is everyone for himself. Whether they have money or not or are in dirty clothes that smell. Can we hug that person and show them the love of Jesus?

Everyone is looking for something. Most people know that a church is supposed to be a place of refuge. The church's mission is to help people. If a Christian would open up their hearts to the ones who need help, give love and begin to show by example what Jesus was talking about when he said, "In as much as ye have done it unto the least of these, ye have done it unto me," {Matthew 25:40} we would see a lot of changes come about in this world. We would see many people changed and the church would once again be the helping station of ministering to hurting and lost souls. She could once again lift her head high and take her rightful place as the perfect example of what the Bride of Christ is suppose to be.

We are to be a Holy church, God said, "Be ye holy as I am holy." We are not to give the world cause to call us unholy. We are to follow God's example in everything we do. If you're not sure what to do in a situation, get out the word or pray and ask God. No time in the history of the church has it been such an exciting time to serve God as now. It is time for the rapture of the church to take place. We should be trying to see everyone saved before it is too late. After the rapture of the church it will only be the ones that know some things about the word and what will be taking place to be saved, if they have taken the mark of the beast it will be too late for them, they will be lost with no chance for repentance.

In I Thessalonians 5:17 God said, "To pray without ceasing." If we are doing this, the whole time, we would see a revived church for we would have no time to complain or worry about things. Doing this in your prayer language or in the Spirit always helps shields the fiery darts of Satan against you for you will have a hedge prayed around you continually. I believe the church is getting ready for a great come back. God said in Acts 2: 17–18, "'And it shall come to pass in the last days,' saith God, 'I will pour out of my Spirit upon all flesh: and sons and your daughters shall prophesy, and your young men shall see visions, and your old men shall dream, dreams: And on my servants and on my handmaidens I will pour out in those days of my Spirit; and they shall prophesy.'" The church is going to be mighty again, with or without us. We can't stop it nor can Satan stop it, for whether he likes it or not. Jesus is alive and well.

God said, "He is coming back for a church without spot or wrinkle," a church on fire for the things of God, not a lukewarm church. In Revelation 3:16, God says, "Because you were lukewarm and neither cold not hot, He would spew us out of His mouth." You can't accomplish anything if you are half hearted about it. You have to want to do it; that is what He wants, hot on fire, excited about his church. Every service we go to we should go in prepared to meet God and be in his holy presence. We should go from glory to glory. Every service should be exciting. This is where we come to meet with God.

In the Old Testament, when the children of Israel were being lead by God, it was with a cloud. When they set up the tabernacle {or tent}, the cloud of God {the Sheckinah Glory of God} would descend on the tent. They couldn't leave till it lifted. Can you imagine if we went to church and every time we went the Sheckinah cloud of glory would descend on our service and we couldn't leave until it lifted? I would love to be in God's glory each and every service I attend. We today wouldn't know what it was if it did fall on us. We need to get in the word to find out how to have the cloud of God to set on our churches and not lift till He was ready. We need to pray daily for this to happen to us today. It does occasionally if you have the opportunity to ever read *The God Chasers* written by Tommy Tinney, please do so. That is exactly what happened to the church he was going to minister in. This is what God wants for all his churches not just some on occasion. We need to begin to chase after God so determined to see what is completely God's will that he can catch us in the process so we can go into the Holy of Holies where the Sheckinah glory of God resides, fall on the mercy seat and receive God's grace to fulfill God's will for our lives, so we can take many souls home when the time comes. This is the real church God created in the beginning.

CHAPTER 4
Steps and Conditions

Now I am going to share a few steps or rules, and the conditions that God put in his word for us to learn by.

We must go to Ezekiel chapter 43–47. It gives us an insight into this. Some I have already discussed. In chapter 43, we see where God said his church was defiled. Ezekiel talks about God taking him into the courts to see this vision. God compares his church now to the temple of old. It was in three parts, the outer court or porch, the inner court or sanctuary, and the Holy of Holies, where God dwells.

First, we are going to discuss the "Outer Court" or Porch. This is outside the church doors. Back when I was a kid, the porch was where you left you dirty shoes or muddy things so you wouldn't track dirt into the house. The same is true here. God's outer court was where you left your dirty sins so as not to bring them into the inner court. Back then the ordinary person could not enter into the inner court only the priest could do that. Today we can all come into the inner court or sanctuary bringing all the baggage that we carry with us.

The first thing we must understand is for us to have gotten this far in step one is God put us on someone's heart to pray for our salvation. Step two is God has already dealt with our hearts for us to come to church to learn about him. God is now able to prepare your heart for the cleansing and changing that is to take place now in your life. With some people, God takes all of our bad habits at one time but with others he only takes one thing at a time for only he knows what you can handle and what you can't. The word says he will only give you what you can bear and not any more. These are steps in your conversion to being born again.

After I gave my life to Christ, I had a dream one night that I was peeling wallpaper off a wall. Some of the paper came off in long strips but some I had to pick at for a long time to get just a little strip or a piece off. This is the way God was showing me he was changing me. Some habits would go quickly like in one long strip of paper and other habits I would have to let him really work at before I was willing to totally give them up to him and quit doing them, I was one he didn't take all my bad things at one time, it was over a course of time.

Once you give all your cares and burdens to God and

lay your life on his alter of forgiveness and mercy, he will now teach you all about the rest of the steps and conditions you will need to serve him. So many of us never pay any attention to his steps or rules nor to the conditions he has laid out in the word but he is very serious about them or he would not have them in there. God will not quit or give up on you till all your steps are complete and you are being conformed into his image. The steps we take with God in our growth are like our children take as they learn to walk and grow. It is one step at a time. Sometimes we fall but like a baby we get up and try again. When we do fall, God is there hovering over us to encourage us to get up and do it again. We must learn to pray and read the word so we can grow in that area. How will we know what to do and not to do if we don't read and learn the conditions that go along with the steps? Praying is another condition which we have talked about in a previous chapter, the steps is learning how to pray. Praying is one thing we must do before we come to church to prepare us to enter into his presence during praise and worship. It helps us to leave all the stuff in the outer court rather than bringing it inside. Our attitude is another step in the process of entering in to his presence. We must come before him in reverence and humbleness to receive from him, this is a condition. Our money is another step we must learn about in serving God, earning it is what we do, and the condition to that is he requires ten percent of your wages, then your time, then servitude, and spending time with him.

Another step we must discuss is communion. This is God's covenant with his church. The condition to this is we must repent and take it with a pure heart. Are we really repentative before God? Are we taking his broken body [the bread] and his blood [the wine] with a pure heart and mind, or is it just a ritual we do? This is a sacred and holy part of serving God and we treat it so lightly. God says we are offering a polluted sacrifice on his holy alter if we take it unworthily.

I believe God is saying now, "People wake up, I am a Holy God. I will not put up with all the sin you are bringing into my house much longer. I want my people who are called by my name to take measure." The word says, "That they maybe ashamed and begin to do what is Holy before me and repent before it is too late." God forbid we being so stubborn a people that we ignore what God is saying through Ezekiel to us today. We bring every conceivable thing inside his house. He is saying these things belong in the outer court not in my sanctuary. Remember when God got mad about everyone selling inside His temple. [Jn.2:14–16] Jesus made a whip, went inside, over turned the tables, scattered everything, and told them his father's house was not a house of merchandise but a house of prayer. These things were an abomination before God.

God help us to understand how serious we need to be about your house and the "Outer Court" of your church and our lives, that we may learn and follow your rules or steps for our lives and the conditions you have set forth in the Word of God that we may enter into your presence. Remember when you go through the doors of the church into His sanctuary, it is to worship Him. Every door leading into God's Inner court or sanctuary should have a sign posted, Enter to Worship.

CHAPTER 5
The Inner Court or Sanctuary

We have discussed in a previous section about the outer court and what not to bring into the sanctuary of God. Now, we will discuss what the "Inner Court" is and what God expects from us, so we can enter into the Holy of Holies.

To enter in, we must first prepare. This is spending time with God, get in the word, and study it, and by praying.

In Ezekiel 46, God talks about the Inner Court. He said, "We must prepare daily to be with Him." The word says, "Seek Him early that you may find Him" (Proverbs 8:17). Now to come into God's presence or to have the Shechinah Glory of God to come into the sanctuary we must prepare our hearts, and our spirits. All the junk of the world can't come inside with us. God says, "When we enter in we must give of ourselves an oblation offering" {unblemished}. Give voluntarily all that we have, holding nothing back. God didn't hold anything back from us when he sent his son. His offering or sacrifice was unblemished to us and voluntary.

We must be like the Psalmist David in Psalms 51:10–12, "Create in me a clean heart, O God; and renew a right spirit within me. Cast me not away from thy presence; and take not thy Holy Spirit from me. Restore unto me the joy of thy salvation; and uphold me with thy free spirit."

We cannot come into church with dirty garments on and try to work up the Holy Spirit. We must be in the right spirit. We can do nothing on our own. We must lay ourselves on the altar of God, put on the garments of praise and truly begin to worship God in Spirit and Truth.

The sanctuary of God should be the shining glory of God. The sanctuary is where we come to meet with God. In chapter 46: 9, it says, "What ever door you enter by, you must leave by another door." When we come into God's presence wanting to praise and worship Him, we should indeed be changed. We should leave different than when we entered in. No one, if they truly meet God face to face, can remain the same. We must come expecting a difference. Look at Paul when he met Jesus on the road to Damascus. He was never the same. Thank God, or we gentiles would not have had the opportunity to be saved, for salvation was for God's chosen people, but because they rejected Jesus and crucified him, only then did God choose a man called

Ezekiel's Vision of the Church Today

Saul of Tarsus to preach the word to us and give us the right to called the sons of God. We may be only grafted into the branch of God through adoption by Jesus, but we are still saved by grace through the blood of Jesus.

If the Holy Ghost sent tongues of fire to set on each one of us today like at Pentecost, and the tongues of fire began to dance across the roof of the church and the Sheckinah Glory of God fell inside the church, we would begin to have a revival like no one has ever seen before. Truly entering into his presence praising and worshiping him, wanting this so badly will start something so powerful in our churches across this land, it would make everything else look like a Sunday school picnic. We should be like Joshua in Exodus 33:11. When we enter into his presence, we should never want to leave, but to drink of this water where we will be thirsty no more.

Ezekiel 47, it talks about the waters of the Holy Spirit. It says it comes from the forefront of the house and it runs down the side of the altar. You must first come to the altar of God and make sure everything is right with you and God so you can enter into this flow. Now it talks about this man {an angel} measuring the waters that is flowing out of the house. As he measured, it was a thousand cubits, which is, one-third of a mile and it was up to the ankles.

Now up to the ankles is not very deep but some people won't go very deep with God, only far enough to get their feet wet, afraid of what God will expect of them. This could be a cleansing time for you. God is trying to see if you desire a closer walk with him or you only want the benefits of the word and not the commitment that goes with it. This step measures us to see our depth and how far we want to go in him. No more straddling the fence, you must choose whose side your on and how far you want to go in God. You cannot serve two masters {God and Mammon, who is Satan}. You must get rooted and grounded in the word so Satan can't feed you lies and steal the truth of the word from you.

Again, the man measured and it was to his knees. This is a little deeper, for some it could be times or periods of restoration for us and our churches. Taking us back to a time of fullness and release in the spirit that we knew at one time but seem to have lost along the way. God said in the beginning we are to measure the pattern in Ezekiel. 43:10. In verse 11 it says, "If they be ashamed of all that they have done, shew them the form of the house and the fashion there of, and the goings out thereof and the comings in there of, and all the forms there of, and all the ordinances there of, and all the forms there of, and all the laws there of, and write them in their sight, that they may keep the whole form there of, and all the ordinances there of, and do them." Wading in the water and being measured by God is not easy. Sometimes frightening but to go all the way we must follow what God has laid down in his word.

Then the man measured to the loins. This is part way with God still not giving every part of their lives to God, still holding things back. They must turn over every part of their lives so God can restore it all to them, taking them deeper and deeper with him.

You could be stopping the richest blessings of your lives. We must start to follow the steps and conditions God has laid out for us. In Ezekiel 43:13, if there is exact measurements for the altar and everything God had man make, what makes us think he is not exact in how he says the house of God should operate first the natural and then the spiritual?

Again, the man measured and it's a river, one you had to swim in. This is what God wants His church to be today, so full of the spirit of God, we get drunk on it. Oh, to go to church where the praising and worshiping is so sweet we can swim in the spirit and not worry about time. When it is over we are like Moses, we shine so much from God's glory and being in the presence of God we must cover our faces because we blind people.

The praising and worshiping part is very important in the church, to the entering in of His presence. If a lot of the churches would let go, and let God do in their services what He wants, we could change the world. The praise and worship leads us into the time of the Word of God. Sometimes praising God will do more in a service through song and the music than the preaching. When the Spirit of God begins to speak through His music, it will sometimes melt the hardest of hearts and bring about conviction by the Holy Spirit, and get people saved.

Why churches and people think it is not important is beyond me. What do they think we are going to do when we get to heaven? We won't need the word of God preached to us, there will be no sinners there; all we will do is Praise and Worship God. God wants us to practice while we're here. Most churches have a format to follow, two or three hymns, then the Word, then go home. If we allowed the Spirit of God to flow in our churches today, through the Praise and Worship and truly mean it before God, by the time the Word came, the whole church would be so full of God's presence we would never want to leave. This is when the churches will begin to fill up and souls will be saved. Even if we must walk alone with God and no one else stands with us, we must go with the moving of God within us. Don't become stagnant; God calls this Salty Marshes. Everything in and around them are dead or decayed. If we stand still long enough we also become dead or decayed. We must keep on moving and growing in God.

God says in Ezekiel 47: 1–13, that if we truly praise and worship Him, and the church and his people get right before him, everything around these waters will be healed, no more desert places, dried up and ready to blow away. Everything shall live and we shall not fade for we shall have the meat of the Word also. "We will be matured in Christ," not babies in the word but able to bring forth new fruit and we will have the leaf for medicine, God promises health to us, and all because it, the waters of the Spirit, issued out of the "Inner Court" or Sanctuary and we are to be consumed by it. Are we being consumed by the Spirit of God?

In verse 13 it says, "This river of water shall be the border, whereby we shall inherit the land," {Canaan}. The land that flows with milk and honey. When we are completely consumed and go all the way with God, then will we enter into the Holy of Holies. I don't know if we can go any farther than this but let us all try. When we give everything to God in our lives then we can start to receive our inheritances now. If we leave out any of these steps and conditions that God has given us, we will never be able to enter completely into His presence.

Remember, we enter the Inner Court or Sanctuary to Worship God.

CHAPTER 6
The Unfaithful Priests

Now I have talked about the outer court and the inner court and what the people have to begin to do, leaving things outside the sanctuary, and entering the sanctuary for worship.

Now I will go one step or one condition farther, the Priests, or Pastors, requirements for coming into God's presence to see the Sheckinah Glory of God fall on the churches today.

Ezekiel talks a little bit about these Priests and Pastors, in chapter 44 saying, "All were to be of the lineage of the Levities." He talks about some that are faithful and some that are unfaithful. Let's discuss the unfaithful first. They are the ones that are Levities but are of the lineage we will call the Abiathar Priests. Now Abiathar was a priest during the time of King David. He and a priest called Zadok held the duties together. Abiathar was of the lineage of Eli. Abiathar was at one time a faithful priest, until he got his eyes off of God and began to look to the natural.

In I Kings 1, we see where David is old and ready to die. God had said when he died Solomon would reign and would build God's house. We see where one of David's sons, Adonijah was his name, decided on his own that he wanted to be King and since David was ready to die and had as yet not given his kingdom over, Adonijah decided not to wait but tried to steal the throne. Now Abiathar, being high priest, knew the throne was to go to Solomon but he got his eyes on the things of this earth rather than on God's promises and so he backed Adonijah, wanting to be on the winning side. You know, pleasing self and people rather than God, thinking he might rise even higher if he advocated the same things as Adonijah and might prosper quit well with him, when he really should have stayed on God's side, not the world's side.

We see, today, a lot of pastors and priests have a concept similar to Abiathar's, people pleasers for prosperities sake. Which means people won't pay tithes if I don't do as they say. "Mr. John Doe is a lawyer and Mr. and Mrs. so and so are doctors, influential people in the community if I don't please them I will lose them and their money to some other church. Now Mrs. so and so has always run the functions, even if she isn't capable she has been here so long, a pillar of the church. We wouldn't want to hurt her feelings even though Miss so and so is far more capable to handle the job and she is who God has chosen. We can't upset the apple cart. I'm sure God will understand considering the circumstances and my reputation as Pastor here is so much more important than seeing the church run by His standards and ordinances." God says, in Ezekiel 44, "He will not make them stop ministering in this church or that church, but because they would not stand up for the pure things of God and they have put on filthy earthly garments. He will lift his hand against them and they shall bear the sin of that church for not teaching their people how to follow God in all kinds of situations and circumstances, trusting God to supply the needs of them and God's church." God said, "They could not come near him because they have sinned and have brought this down on their churches and their people."

In Jeremiah 12:10, it reads, "Many Pastors have destroyed my vineyard, they have trodden my portion under foot, they have made my pleasant portion {place} a desolate wilderness." Look out when your Pastor begins to let people control how the church is run rather than God. If he is not praying for God's will in your church, you will end up with a desolate church.

The Pastor is to be your example of how Jesus wants his

bride to be: pure, holy, walking right before God, not taking advantage of his people. How can we come into God's shining, glorious Sheckinah Glory if the Pastor isn't right before God? He should be seeking God for his church, finding out what is wrong and how to correct it. In Jeremiah 23:1 it says, "Woe be unto the Pastors that destroy and scatter the sheep of my pasture." God is a Holy God. The people that are in those positions are to be Holy Pastors. They are to care for the church and their flock the way Jesus and God the Father cares. It is the Bride of Christ. God is not coming for an unclean, unholy bride. "Woe to the Pastors who treat her as a harlot," being bought by the people and the earthly influences they have. Will this help you if God really lifts his hand against your church? A few years ago some very big named pastors and evangelists were judged very severely by God for the things they were doing. When it all came out, a lot of churches were hurt and a lot of sheep were scattered because of pastors getting their eyes on man and his influences rather than what God wants.

In Ezekiel 34:2, 4 God says, "Woe be to the shepherds who do feed themselves! Should not the shepherds feed the flocks? The diseased have ye not strengthened, neither have ye healed that which was sick, neither have ye bound up that which was broken, neither have ye brought again that which was driven away, neither have ye sought that which was lost; but with force and with cruelty have ye ruled them." We think we are doing a fine job as long as everyone is happy and the church is run the way they want it run.

What kind of manmade idols have we put in God's house? What and who have we been bowing to? Pastors, we need to lay the idols of this world down and not allow man to influence us. Start being the "Man of God" we were called to be, begin to seek God's will and become the faithful once again rather than the unfaithful, and see what God will do. It may not always be popular with the people but if God is happy and you know it is right, God will begin to lift you up, not man, even if you lose a few people in the beginning. Leave it to God this is better than maybe missing out.

God says, "If you gain the whole world and lose your soul, what have you profited." {Matthew 16:26}

Back in I Kings chapter 1, God still had on the throne whom he chose. Zadok the faithful Priest was there for the crowning. When it is all over, will you still be of the lineage of Abiathar the unfaithful priests and be cast out of the kingdom worthy of death and total separation from God? Remember, God is a just God and eternity is forever. Is it worth it, pastors?

CHAPTER 7
The Zadok Priests

Now we shall discuss the faithful Priests. The word talks about them in Ezekiel 44:15–31; they are the Pastors that are left when everyone else has given up. He is still faithful to the calling of God on his life, for he knows where his help comes from, not the people. God says, "These are the ones dressed in linen garments." Now the priests were told to wear linen because it kept them cool and dry. When they went into the Holy of Holies, they were not even permitted to perspire; this was against God's rules or laws pertaining to entering the Holy of Holies. Linen was also white and pure. If we look at this closely we will see that its meaning is still good today. Linen was cool and the pastors are to be cool and confident in God, he will take care of his church. When ministering and dealing with people, they are not to try and have their own way.

The linen was pure white. Aren't our pastors to be the examples of purity and a clean life? They are not to be hot and perspiring from worry but calm and sure in the ways of God. These are the priests and pastors that God can always count on to uphold their office. They are the ones God says is to teach his people the difference between the holy and profane {common}, and cause them to discern between the unclean and the clean. {Ezekiel 44:23}.

A Zadok Pastor is in the Word constantly digging for what God wants them to give his people. They must above all things, please God first and foremost and then try to please the people. If the man of God diligently seeks God's face for his will and runs the church by God's laws and what the word says, he may not always make the most friends but he will always have God's attention.

They must also be prayer warriors for their church, standing in the gap for the people, praying for the sick, encouraging the incurable, seeking the lost sheep as a faithful shepherd. Now if the Pastors aren't right, how can they preach the uncompromising word of God, and how can they lead the people into Praise and Worship and into his Holy presence? They must stand and say, "If God says no, it isn't right, then it is no, sin is sin." It may not be popular but he will be right in God's sight.

In verse 24 of Ezekiel 44, the word says, "They are to stand in judgment in controversy and judge what God would judge." This doesn't mean they are to judge you, it means if there is a controversy in the church and it can't be settled, they take it to God and they have final say in the matter. They find out what God would judge and that is final. They can't do this if they don't spend a lot of time with God. Now, if you are doing wrong or sinning, the Holy Spirit may reveal to the pastor there is a sin being done and they may preach about the sin without ever having known who it is. God knows exactly who you are and what you have done. This may convict you and you can repent of it and make things right with God, or God may tell him who it is and for him to speak to you privately. God will not condone sin in his house; remember, this is the Bride of Christ.

The pastor has the duty to pray over every office in the church. He should know who is to hold offices, who is to teach, sing, usher, hold staff positions and council offices. This is part of his job as shepherd over the church. Even Jesus prayed to the Father before selecting his disciples. As head, it is the pastor's responsibility not to let a wolf in. If he allows a person to hold a position without praying about it, when and if he finds out it is wrong it may be too late to remove them. The damage is already done. Every person who comes inside the church doors and stays as a member, he, the pastor, should go before God with their name and ask what spirit are they of? What gifts do they flow in? What office should they hold if any? Are they sent as intercessors for the body of Christ and the pastor? All these things every good pastor should ask God about. For only God knows everything about a person and only the Holy Spirit can reveal the truth about someone.

A pastor's job is not just preaching a message a couple times a week. He really has an awesome job to perform. I guess that is why God has the five fold ministry already laid out in the word. God has chosen each job carefully so not everyone is a pastor, teacher or prophet. There are people given spiritual gifts and anointed for every job that needs done.

We, the sheep or flock under this shepherd, are to show respect for him and his office. We are to see that they are not in need, in Ezekiel 44:30, it says we are to give our best for them so that God's blessings will rest on our homes. You should make sure they have plenty of food. Do you know how much they spend when they have speakers come to the church and then take then home after the service to provide a meal? Some speakers stay with the pastors the whole time they are speaking at your church. Remember to take some food over to the house. It will really help out. Provide them with a good salary. They earn every penny of it being your shepherd. Have pastor's appreciation day once a year; show them how much you really love them. You take them out to eat once in a while, family included.

Remember we are as liable to God for the care of them and their families, as they are to God for us.

The kind of pastors God is talking about here is really rare. They are men and women after God's own heart. The way they run the church says a lot about how close a walk they have with God. In verse 9–10 in chapter 45 of Ezekiel says, they are to remove violence from the church, which is hatred and unforgiveness, they're to preach against it, for we need a forgiving spirit. The word says if we can't or won't forgive our brothers, the Father won't forgive us. {Matthew 6:14–15} It has no place in the house of God, then he says remove spoil. Tell the people greed has no place in the kingdom of God. Get it out of his house. Remember the law of tithing, and the scripture, "If you gain the whole world and lose your soul, what hath it profited you."

The church is to have just balances, the love of God and the justice of God. It is not all one way. It is the example of God. God is a God of love but he is also a God of wrath. So you must also teach the admonition of the Lord, which is the fear of God, as well as the love of God. There must be a good balance between the two.

The church is to execute justice and judgment. Preach sin is sin, tell the people there is a hell and they could very easily go there. I have heard people say, "God is a loving God and he would not let anyone go to hell." Well, he is also a just God; if you aren't serving him then you are serving Satan. God said, "If you aren't for him you are against him." I don't see much gray matter there. It is pretty black and white. Besides, God doesn't let anyone go to hell; it is your choice where you spend eternity. You decide where you will go.

The pastors that are the lineage of Zadok have a lot riding in them. They will stand before God like everyone else and will answer for how they ran God's church and took care of his people. Their blood could very well be on his hands if he is not faithful to the laws and ordinances of God. The name Zadok means "righteous" and God's pastors are to be exactly that. They are in no way to lead the flock astray or cause them to stumble or fall.

We, as the flock, are to pray for them daily. Remember, Satan will hit them the hardest and usually when they walk through fire we are close behind them. We are not to judge them or any of the flock. I heard a preacher say once, "If they fall, it is usually because we the church dropped them." We quit praying for them and lifting them up daily before God, thinking that someone else was probably praying for them. This is so true and when we do this and become hap hazard about it, we stop the blessings of God in our churches and homes.

If we are on our knees lifting them and the body up before the throne, we would have no time for anything else to enter into our spirits. Let us thank God daily, that we have pastors that are faithful to the calling of God. They, indeed, are a blessing from God to us. Let us all start being from the lineage of Zadok, righteous above all else. Remember to enter the presence of God they, our pastors, must have on righteous garments also.

CHAPTER 8
Conclusion

Now we can enter into the Holy of Holies, this is being totally consumed by the Holy Spirit of God. God said, "We can come boldly with assurance that he will meet with us if we follow the steps and conditions that He has set down in His word for us to follow."

This book shows how we must go from a defiled and polluted church of today, by His path and directions to the glorious and beautiful Bride He is getting ready to come for. Remember, God is not coming for a dirty and polluted bride, one that acts like a harlot, who links her arms with the world, and thinks it is ok.

God says, "Repent now for the kingdom of heaven is at hand." Each one of us has to work out our own salvation with fear and trembling. Philippians 2:12 You won't be able to get into heaven on someone else's salvation. No one can make you right with God but you. But at all costs let's get right and make heaven our home.

To be the beautiful Bride of Christ, we must put on the garments of praise and of righteousness, and meet every condition that He requires of us so we can inherit the kingdom of God and all its blessings. You know so much of your walk will be strictly by faith, but to miss what God says is waiting for us at journeys end is just not worth it, folks. God says, "If we gain the whole world and lose our soul it has profited us nothing." Let's not give our salvation away, nor sell it, nor gamble it away. His shed blood at Calvary is so precious, without it we would have no chance for salvation or the entering in of his presence.

Let's read the word and ask God to open it up to us, teach us exactly what it means chapter and verse. Let's know the directions by heart. Ask Him to write it on our hearts that we would not sin against Him. The journey is not that much longer. Time is running out. The signs of the coming of the Lord are at hand. Make sure you know what they are, so you can run the race to the end. Let us lay down the carnal and pick up the spiritual and gain the prize at the end that will make anything here on earth seem like a pauper owned it. To finally see the face of the Lord and Savior that died for me, to see the love He has for us, the peace beyond measure that awaits us. I'm like Paul sometimes; I would like to leave but my time isn't yet. I, like you, must wait till my time comes to go home. I pray it will be in the rapture with all the other saints. What a day that will be when my Jesus I will see.

When the shout comes and the trumpet sounds, will you hear it today and leave with us or will you look around and say, "Oh God! I thought I was ready and I didn't make it." I have a poem titled "Twas the night before Jesus came"; it is very relevant in getting the meaning across.

TWAS THE NIGHT BEFORE JESUS CAME

Twas the night before Jesus came and all through the house
Not a creature was praying, not one in the house.
Their Bibles were lain on the shelf without care
In hopes that Jesus would not come there.

The children were dressing to crawl into bed,
Not once ever kneeling or bowing a head.
And Mom in her rocker with baby on her lap
Was watching the Late Show while I took a nap.

When out of the East there arose such a clatter,
I sprang to my feet to see what was the matter.
Away to the window I flew like a flash
Tore open the shutters and threw up the sash!

When what to my wondering eyes should appear
But angels proclaiming that Jesus was here
With a light like the sun sending forth a bright ray
I knew in a moment this must be THE DAY!

The light of His face made me cover my head
It was Jesus! Returning just like He had said.
And though I possessed worldly wisdom and wealth,
I cried when I saw Him in spite of myself.

In the Book of Life which He held in His hand.
Was written the name of every saved man.
He spoke not a word as He searched for my name;
When He said "It's not here" my head hung in shame.

The people whose names had been written with love
He gathered to take to His Father above.
With those who were ready He rose without a sound
While all the rest were left standing around.

I fell to my knees, but it was too late;
I had waited too long and thus sealed my fate.
I stood and I cried as they rose out of sight;
Oh, if only I had been ready tonight.

(Author unknown)

There is nothing on this earth that is worth missing the rapture or the call to go home to be with Lord and all the family. You must, at all costs know His conditions and follow them. It will save your soul. You will spend an eternity with God. If not, you will have total separation from God and spend an eternity with Satan. It is your choice.

I pray now that you have read this book you will begin to study His Word. Find a church that preaches the complete Word of God, don't settle for anything less. If you know the Word, then you will not be fooled by a church or person into believing something that is false. I pray that if you don't know God as your personal Savior, now is the time to ask Him to forgive you of your sins and to come into your heart to be Lord and master of your life from now on till eternity. Lets all go home together to the marriage supper of the lamb.

If you have never asked Jesus to come into your heart and abide there forever, now is the time. It is easy, just pray to the Lord.

Father, please forgive me of any and all sins that I may have committed, knowingly or unknowingly and please come into my heart. Help me to live for you the way I am supposed to. Help me to find a church to go to that will teach me the uncompromising word of God. Help me to come home to you when my time on this earth is done, to the marriage supper of the lamb.

I pray this book has helped you to see what the Lord is saying about His Bride, the church. He has laws and commandments to follow. He put them in the word so we could know them and live by them, it was no different with the children of Israel. The Word never changes, nor does God, what He put in the Word is never changing, the covenant He made with the children of old is the same covenant we have with Him today.

Remember when we enter the church doors, we enter to worship, this is where our Father has asked us to come to meet with Him.

When we leave, we exit to serve. This life of ours is to be given to help others. We are to serve the masses and tell them about Jesus. Let us be the uncompromising Bride of Christ, and live a life someone would want to copy.

May God richly bless your life. I hope to meet you one day, in heaven.